D0773057

# STATE
# CONSTITUTIONAL
# CONVENTIONS

# STATE CONSTITUTIONAL CONVENTIONS, REVISIONS, AND AMENDMENTS, 1959-1976
## A Bibliography

A Supplement to
*State Constitutional Conventions,
From Independence to the Present Union, 1776-1959,*
compiled by Cynthia E. Browne,
and *State Constitutional Conventions, 1959-1975,*
compiled by Susan Rice Yarger

*compiled by*
BONNIE CANNING

*introduction by*
RICHARD H. LEACH
*Professor of Political Science,
Duke University*

GREENWOOD PRESS
Westport, Connecticut • London, England

**Library of Congress Cataloging in Publication Data**

Canning, Bonnie.
  State constitutional conventions, revisions, and amendments, 1959-1976.

  "A supplement to State constitutional conventions, from independence to the present Union, 1776-1959, compiled by Cynthia E. Browne, and State constitutional conventions, 1959-1975, compiled by Susan Rice Yarger."
  Includes bibliographic references and index.
  1. Constitutional conventions—United States—States—Bibliography. 2. Constitutions, State—United States—Bibliography. I. Browne, Cynthia E. State constitutional conventions from independence to the completion of the present Union, 1776-1959. II. Yarger, Susan Rice. State constitutional conventions, 1959-1975. III. Title.
KF4501.B76 suppl            016.342'73'024            76-57843
ISBN 0-8371-9487-3

Copyright © 1977 by Greenwood Press, Inc.

Library of Congress Catalog Card Number: 76-57843
ISBN: 0-8371-9487-3

First published in 1977

Greenwood Press, Inc.
51 Riverside Avenue, Westport, Connecticut 06880

Printed in the United States of America

# Contents

# Preface

*State Constitutional Conventions, Revisions and Amendments, 1959-1976* is the third in a series of bibliographies of official materials, published and unpublished, which document state constitutional formation and revision. It complements and expands *State Constitutional Conventions from Independence to the Completion of the Present Union, 1776-1959: A Bibliography*, compiled by Cynthia E. Browne, and *State Constitutional Conventions, 1959-1975: A Bibliography*, compiled by Susan Rice Yarger.

*State Constitutional Conventions, Revisions, and Amendments, 1959-1976* cites official documents, reports, minutes, and background studies for the following:

1) states that held constitutional conventions and brought the results of their efforts to the electorate regardless of the outcome,
2) states that revised their constitution through processes other than a convention.

The states included in this bibliography are California, Delaware, Florida, Kentucky, Louisiana, New Jersey, Texas, Washington, and Wisconsin.

Due to the recency of the Louisiana and Texas conventions, and technical problems in identifying and acquiring materials, the documents for Louisiana, Texas, Florida, and New Jersey supplement the materials in the Yarger bibliography.

Materials for each state are generally arranged in chronological order by issuing agency. Bibliographic arrangement varies somewhat from state to state, however, reflecting the particular approach to constitutional revision of the individual state.

All documents cited in this bibliography are available on archival quality microfiche. Every effort was made to include all relevant documents. Due to the fugitive and elusive nature of this material, however, the publisher cannot guarantee an *absolutely complete* set of documents for each state. The user can be assured that the bibliography and fiche collection make up the *most comprehensive* collection in existence of such materials for the states covered. Some materials were never released for publication or distribution. In other cases, only single copies of reports were prepared, and they could not be released from the state archives.

The publisher would like to thank the Advisory Commission on Intergovernmental Relations, the National Municipal League, Legis 50/The Center for Legislative Improvement, the Louisiana Constitutional Convention Records Commission, the Wisconsin Legislative Reference Library, the University of Washington (state) Law Library, the Florida State University Political Research Institute, the University of Florida Public Administration Clearing Service, the Texas Legislative Reference Library, the Texas State Library, the Texas Advisory Commission of Intergovernmental Relations, the Legislative Council of Delaware, the California State Library, the Los Angeles County Law Library, and the Institute of Governmental Studies, University of California at Berkeley. Their generous cooperation made this project possible.

Bonnie Canning
Bowie, Maryland

# Introduction

Action to update state constitutions so as to make them the viable instruments the states need to enable them to retain and develop the important areas of government over which they have jurisdiction in the American system of government has been a dominant theme in American politics and government ever since World War II. Indeed, as Albert L. Sturm noted in *The Book of the States 1976-1977,* "Since midcentury, more official attention has been given to revising and modernizing state constitutions than during any comparable period since the Reconstruction era . . . effective constitutional reform [has been achieved] in approximately one-third of the States during the last two decades. . . ."[1] Sturm's observation suggests that reform is still to be accomplished in the remaining states, but in many, movements for change are already in some stage of development. The task of constitutional adaptation is a continuing one, however; it will never be finished. Not only do the social and economic conditions underlying government continue to require accommodation as they alter over time, but improvements and innovations in the process of government continue to be generated. No part of the governmental process is as important as constitution-making because of the basic adherence of the American people to the concept of government by the rule of law. Thus knowledge of the ongoing constitutional process is required on a regular basis

---

1. Albert L. Sturm, "State Constitutions and Constitutional Revision, 1974-1975," *The Book of the States 1976-1977.* Lexington, Ky., The Council of State Governments, 1976, p. 162.

over time, so that both the people and the actors on the fifty
state governmental stages can be apprised of directions and
trends, as well as of alternatives and the factors leading to
decisions, in the fundamental law supporting them all. It has
not always been easy to acquire that knowledge. With fifty
states, each autonomous in the exercise of its constituent
power, there is no uniform method of approaching and deal-
ing with constitutional change. Such change is ordinarily secured
by one or a combination of three methods: proposal by the
state legislature (all the states), use of the constitutional initia-
tive (17 states), and reliance on a constitutional convention
(41 state constitutions specifically provide for calling constitutional conventions). In a number of states, constitutional
commissions are employed as study and recommendatory
bodies. Whatever method or combination of methods is used,
a great deal of preparatory work accompanies usage. For
many years the large portion of that work which was ephemeral
was lost to subsequent scholarship and understanding. Bibliographies of official reports and documents were often main-
tained, and some of them were quite complete, but other
material, equally important in the final analysis, was not re-
corded at all. The American policy system generally permits
inputs from a wide range of sources, and this is as true of
constitutions as of less basic aspects of the governmental
process. The material on constitutional change—which has
been increasing steadily over the years as public interest in the
subject has expanded—thus came to include even more un-
official inputs, and for the most part, these went unrecorded.

Greenwood Press has begun to fill that void. First in its
50-state review of material utilized by state constitutional
conventions between 1776 and 1959 (*State Constitutional
Conventions 1776-1959. A Bibliography,* compiled by Cynthia
Browne and published in 1973) and then in its subsequent
volume of the same title covering the 18 states which had held
constitutional conventions in the period 1959-1975 (*State
Constitutional Conventions. A Bibliography,* compiled by
Susan Rice Yarger and published in 1976), it has, through

diligent research and analysis in libraries and on site in state capitals, begun to make accessible references to *all* the pertinent material on constitutional revision. Every item listed has been individually checked for relevance and accuracy of citation. The current volume in the series (*State Constitutional Conventions, Amendments, and Revisions, 1959-1976,* compiled by Bonnie Canning, published in 1977) covers nine states in which constitutional revision has taken place in recent years, but which, for technical reasons, were not included in the second volume. It was still difficult to get at and authenticate the materials on Oregon, so that state had to be omitted. The most recent volume is a slim one, but it makes another significant contribution in making available references to the important background studies that underlie so much of modern constitution-making.

Greenwood Press is to be lauded both for its publications to date and for its determination to continue the series with biennial volumes. Because of the care with which these bibliographies have been developed, they constitute a unique asset for scholars and for citizens interested in and concerned about state constitutional development.

Richard H. Leach
Professor of Political Science
Duke University

# STATE CONSTITUTIONAL CONVENTIONS

# General Publications

GP-1    Legis 50/ The Center for Legislative Improvement (formerly, Citizens' Conference on State Legislatures). *A Bibliography on State Constitutions and Constitutional Revision: 1945-1975.* Compiled by Dr. Albert L. Sturm, edited by Kristin Hall. Englewood, Colorado, August 1975.
39 p.

GP-2    (Governors') Committee on Constitutional Revision and Governmental Reorganization. Preliminary Report. (n.p.), 1968 (?).
iv, 145 p.

GP-3    Governors' Committee on Constitutional Revision and Governmental Reorganization. State-By-State Summary of Constitutional Revision and Governmental Reorganization: January 1, 1963 to June 30, 1967. Prepared by staff, Department of Political Science, University of Washington. Seattle, January 1968.
143 p.

# California

Note: The order of the entries in this bibliography is based on the bibliographic arrangement of *Report on the Materials of Constitutional Revision Commission Relating to Provisions in California Constitution Recommended or Endorsed by Commission* [Ca 23]

[Ca 23]
California. Legislature. Joint Rules Committee.
Report on the Materials of Constitutional Revision Commission Relating to Provisions in California Constitution Recommended or Endorsed by Commission. Prepared by J. Gould. (n.p.), December 1974.
147 p.

[Ca 24]
Englebert, Ernest A., and Gunnell, John G.
State Constitutional Revision in California. Los Angeles, April 1961.
viii, 68 p.

[Ca 25]
California. Assembly Interim Committee on Constitutional Amendments.
Report to the California Legislature. Sacramento, November 15, 1960.
60 p.

[Ca 26]
California. Assembly Interim Committee on Constitutional Amendments.
Report to the California Legislature. Parts I & II. Sacramento, January 7, 1963.
49 p., 113 p.

[Ca 34]
California. Assembly Interim Committee on Constitutional Amendments.
Special Report on Constitutional Revision. Sacramento, 1966.
33 p.

[Ca 27]
California. Assembly Interim Committee on Constitutional Amendments.
Final Report: Constitutional Revision in California. Sacramento, January 1967.
103 p.

[Ca 28]
California. Assembly Interim Committee on Constitutional Amendments.
  Final Report: Revision of the California Constitution - Phase II. Sacramento,
March 1968.
x, 81 p., 68 p.

[Ca 29]
California. Assembly Interim Committee on Constitutional Amendments.
  Special Report on Constitutional Revision. Sacramento, January 1969.
45 p.

[Ca 30]
California. Constitution Revision Commission.
  Progress Report to the State Legislature. San Francisco, October 1965.
40 p.

[Ca 31]
California. Constitution Revision Commission.
  Proposed Revision of the California Constitution. San Francisco, February 1966.
212 p.

[Ca 32]
California. Constitution Commission.
  Proposed Revision of the California Constitution. San Francisco, 1968.
125 p.

[Ca 58]
California. Constitution Revision Commission.
  Proposed Revision of the California Constitution.
Parts 1-6. San Francisco, 1970-1971. Part 1 - Introduction.
27 p.

[Ca 59]
———. Part 2 - Articles II, XIV, XV, XXI, XXIII, XXVII, XXXIV.
73 p.

[Ca 60]
———. Part 3 - Articles XVI, XX, XXVI.
52 p.

[Ca 61]
———. Part 4 - Articles IX, X.
40 p.

[Ca 62]
———. Part 5 - Articles I, XX, XXII.
59 p.

[Ca 63]
———. Part 6 - Articles XIII and Revised California Constitution.
137 p.

[Ca 35A]
California. Constitution Revision Commission.
    Article I: Declaration of Rights. Background Study 1. (n.p.), 1969.
36 p.

[Ca 35B]
———. Background Study 2.
23 p.

[Ca 35C]
———. Background Study 3.
67 p.

[Ca 35D]
———. Background Study 4.
35 p.

[Ca 36A]
California. Constitution Revision Commission.
    Article II: Elections and Suffrage. Background Study 1. (n.p.), 1965.
65 p.

[Ca 36B]
———. Background Study 2. 1966.
47 p.

[Ca 36C]
———. Background Study 3. 1967.
25 p.

[Ca 36D]
———. Background Study 4. 1968.
6 p.

[Ca 37]
California. Constitution Revision Commission.
    Article III: Separation of Powers. Background Study. (n.p.), April 1965.
7 p.

[Ca 38A]
    Article IV: Legislative. Background Study. 1965.
54 p.

[Ca 38B]
———. Background Study.
13 p.

[Ca 38C]
———. Background Study.
19 p.

[Ca 38D]
———. Background Study.
8 p.

[Ca 39]
 Article V: Executive Powers. Background Study 4. (n.p.), November 1965.
67 p.

[Ca 40A]
California. Constitution Revision Commission.
 Article IX: Education. Background Study. 1967.
97 p.

[Ca 40B]
———. Background Study.
9 p.

[Ca 40C]
———. Background Study.
15 p.

[Ca 40D]
———. Background Study.
27 p.

[Ca 40E]
———. Background Study.
27 p.

[Ca 40F]
———. Background Study.
30 p.

[Ca 40G]
———. Background Study.
12 p.

[Ca 40H]
———. Background Study.
79 p.

[Ca 40I]
———. Background Study.
4 p.

[Ca 41A]
California. Constitution Revision Commission.
 Article X: State Institutions and Public Buildings. Background Study 1. (n.p.), 1965.
7 p.

[Ca 41B]
———. Background Study 2.
8 p.

[Ca 41C]
———. Background Study 3.
8 p.

[Ca 41D]
———. Background Study 4.
v.p.

[Ca 42A]
California. Constitution Revision Commission.
  Article XI: Local Government. Background Study. (n.p.), 1967.
iii, 144 p.

[Ca 42B]
———. Background Study.
xii, 420 p.

[Ca 43A]
California. Constitution Revision Commission.
  Article XII: Corporations and Public Utilities. Background Study. San Francisco, 1966.
135 p.

[Ca 43B]
———. Background Study. 1967.
viii, 42 p., 349 p.

[Ca 44A]
California. Constitution Revision Commission.
  Article XIII: Revenue & Taxation. Background Study 1. San Francisco, 1969.
30 p.

[Ca 44B]
———. Background Study 2.
80 p.

[Ca 44C]
———. Background Study 3.
70 p.

[Ca 44D]
———. Background Study 4.
19 p.

[Ca 44E]
———. Background Study 5.
29 p.

[Ca 44F]
———. Background Study 6.
9 p.

[Ca 44G]
———. Background Study 7.
15 p.

[Ca 44H]
———. Background Study 8.
27 p.

[Ca 44I]
———. Background Study 9.
23 p.

[Ca 44J]
———. Background Study 10.
30 p.

[Ca 44K]
———. Background Study 11.
34 p.

[Ca 45A]
California. Constitution Revision Commission.
   Article XIV: Water & Water Rights. Background Study 1. San Francisco, 1968.
38 p.

[Ca 45 B]
———. Background Study 2.
9 p.

[Ca 46A]
California. Constitution Revision Commission.
   Article XV: Harbor Frontages. Background Study 1. San Francisco, 1968.
21 p.

[Ca 46B]
———. Background Study 2.
19 p.

[Ca 47A]
California. Constitution Revision Commission.
   Article XVI: State Debt. Background Study 1. San Francisco, 1969.
44 p.

[Ca 47B]
———. Background Study 2.
5 p.

[Ca 47C]
———. Background Study 3.
40 p.

[Ca 47D]
———. Background Study 4.
60 p.

[Ca 47E]
———. Background Study 5.
14 p.

[Ca 47F]
———. Background Study 6.
13 p.

[Ca 48]
California. Constitution Revision Commission.
    Article XVII: Land Ownership. Background Study Number 4. San Francisco, 1966.
10 p.

[Ca 65]
California. Constitution Revision Commission.
    Article XVIII: Amending and Revising the Constitution. Committee's Minutes, Reports, and Background Study 1. San Francisco, 1966.
85 p.

[Ca 49A]
California. Constitution Revision Commission.
    Article XVIII: Amending and Revising the Constitution. Background Study 2. San Francisco, 1966.
45 p.

[Ca 49B]
———. Background Study 3.
51 p.

[Ca 49C]
———. Background Study 4.
53 p.

[Ca 49D]
———. Background Study 5.
57 p.

[Ca 49E]
———. Background Study 6.
58 p.

[Ca 49F]
———. Background Study 7.
61 p.

[Ca 50A]
California. Constitution Revision Commission.
    Article XX: Miscellaneous. Background Study 1. San Francisco, 1968.
15 p.

[Ca 50B]
———. Background Study 2.
8 p.

[Ca 50C]
———. Background Study 3.
49 p.

[Ca 50D]
———. Background Study 4.
9 p.

[Ca 50E]
———. Background Study 5.
16 p.

[Ca 50F]
———. Background Study 6.
28 p.

[Ca 51]
California. Constitution Revision Commission.
    Article X, Section 1, Paragraph 3: Convict Labor. Background Study. San Francisco, 1970.

[Ca 52]
California. Constitution Revision Commission.
    Article XXI: State Boundaries. Background Study 2. San Francisco, 1968.
17 p.

[Ca 53]
California. Constitution Revision Commission.
    Article XXII: Schedule. Background Study. San Francisco, 1970.
9 p.

[Ca 54]
California. Constitution Revision Commission.
    Article XXIII: Recall. Background Study. San Francisco, 1968.
55 p.

[Ca 55A]
California. Constitution Revision Commission.
    Article XXVI: Motor Vehicles Taxation & Revenues. Background Study 1. San Francisco,
1968.
11p.

[Ca 55B]
———. Background Study 2.
17 p.

[Ca 56A]
California. Constitution Revision Commission.
    Article XXVII: Repeal of Article XXV, Old Age Security and Security for the Blind.
Background Study. San Francisco, 1968.
8 p., 6 p.

[Ca 56B]
———. Background Study 2.
8 p., 6 p.

[Ca 57]
California. Constitution Revision Commission.
    Article XXXIV: Public Housing. Background Study 1. San Francisco, 1968.
18 p.

[Ca 64]
California. Los Angeles City Charter Commission. City Government for the Future.
    Los Angeles, July 1969.
224 p.

# Delaware

[De 18]
Snowden, James H. (Delaware State Senate)
  Constitutional Revision. An address presented at the Eastern Regional
Conference, Council of State Governments. September 9-12, 1969.
2 p.

[De 19]
Supreme Court of the State of Delaware.
  Opinion of the Justices of the Supreme Court in Response to a Question Propounded
by the Governor of Delaware ("Does Article 16, Section 1, of the Delaware Constitution
permit the adoption of an amendment or amendments which would revise the entire Constitution?"). Dover, March 2, 1970.
12 p.

[De 20]
Delaware Constitutional Revision Commission.
  Official Transcript of Proceedings. Dover, March 14, 1968.
76 p.

[De 21]
———. May 16, 1968.
140 p.

[De 22]
———. May 28, 1968.
106 p.

[De 23]
———. June 3, 1968.
134 p.

[De 24]
———. June 14, 1968.
63 p.

[De 25]
———. June 21, 1968.
110 p.

[De 26]
———. July 8, 1968.
112 p.

[De 27]
———. July 15, 1968.
196 p.

[De 28]
———. July 22, 1968.
167 p.

[De 29]
———. July 29, 1968.
134 p.

[De 30]
———. August 5, 1968.
119 p.

[De 31]
———. August 12, 1968.
121 p.

[De 32]
———. August 19, 1968.
109 p.

[De 33]
———. September 9, 1968.
96 p.

[De 34]
———. September 16, 1968.
160 p.

[De 35]
———. September 30, 1968.
93 p.

[De 36]
———. October 7, 1968.
102 p.

[De 37]
———. October 14, 1968.
115 p.

[De 38]
———. October 21, 1968.
138 p.

[De 39]
———. October 28, 1968
112 p.

[De 40]
———. November 11, 1968.
106 p.

[De 41]
———. November 18, 1968.
102 p.

[De 42]
———. November 25, 1968.
215 p.

[De 43]
———. December 2, 1968.
214 p.

[De 44]
———. December 9, 1968.
193 p.

[De 45]
———. December 16, 1968.
146 p.

[De 46]
———. January 6, 1969.
116 p.

[De 47]
———. January 13, 1969.
119 p.

[De 48]
———. January 27, 1969.
93 p.

[De 49]
———. February 3, 1969.
117 p.

[De 50]
———. April 21, 1969.
146 p.

   *NOTE:* April 28, 1969 is missing

[De 51]
———. August 11, 1969.
114 p.

[De 52]
———. August 25, 1969.
155 p.

[De 53]
———. September 3, 1969.
209 p.

[De 54]
———. September 8, 1969.
237 p.

[De 55]
———. September 15, 1969.
280 p.

[De 56]
———. October 6, 1969.

[De 57]
Delaware Constitutional Revision Commission.
  Official Transcript of Proceedings. Public Hearing. Dover, July 8, 1969.
v. p. (95 p.)

[De 58]
———. July 15, 1969.
47 p.

[De 59]
———. July 16, 1969.
v. p. (211 p.)

[De 60]
Delaware, Constitutional Revision Commission.
  (Commentary explaining changes and revision of the Delaware Constitution as proposed
by the Constitutional Revision Commission.) (n.p.), (n.d.).
v. p. (35 p.)

[De 61]
Delaware. Constitution(al) Revision Commission.
  Commentary on the Proposed Constitution: A Side-By-Side Comparison, Present Constitution - Proposed Constitution. Dover, February 1970.
167 p.

[De 62]
Delaware Legislature.
  "An Act proposing an Amendment to the Constitution of the State of Delaware."
Delaware State Senate, 128th General Assembly, First Session - 1975, Senate Bill No. 50,
January 16, 1975.
41 p.

  "An Act prescribing the next general election as the proper occasion for ascertaining
the sense of the people in respect to calling a convention to revise, alter and amend the
Constitution." Delaware State Senate, 128th General Assembly, First Session - 1975,
Senate Bill No. 275, May 6, 1975.
4 p.

  "An Act proposing an amendment to Article XVI of the Constitution of the State of
Delaware, relating to the number of delegates for a constitutional convention." Delaware
State Senate, 128th General Assembly, First Session - 1975, Senate Bill No. 276, May 6, 1975.
1 p.

# Florida

[Fl 27]
Florida. Constitution Revision Commission.
   Selected Bibliography on State Constitutional Revision. Prepared by Albert L. Sturm and the Staff of the Institute of Governmental Research (now Political Research Institute), Florida State University, Tallahassee, January, 1966.
28 p.

[Fl 28]
Florida. Governor.
   Governor LeRoy Collins' Special Message on the Constitution to the Joint Session of the Senate and the House of Representatives of the Florida Legislature in the Chamber of the House of Representatives. Tallahassee, April 1959.
9 p.

[Fl 39]
University of Florida. Public Administration Clearing Service.
   Reapportionment and Other Constitutional Amendments of 1962. By Ruth McQuown. Gainesville, 1962 (Civic Information Series No. 40).
30 p.

[Fl 29]
University of Florida. Public Administration Clearing Service.
   Legislative Power to Revise Constitution/Reorganization of Board of Control and Other Constitutional Amendments of 1964. Prepared by Manning J. Dauer and Gladys M. Kammerer. Gainesville, 1964 (Civic Information Series No. 43).
ii, 28 p.

[Fl 30]
University of Florida. Public Administration Clearing Service.
   A New Method for Discipline and Removal of Judges and Other Amendments of 1966. Prepared by Gladys M. Kammerer. Gainesville, 1966 (Civic Information Series No. 46).

[Fl 32]
University of Florida. Public Administration Clearing Service.
   Should Florida Adopt the Proposed 1968 Constitution? By Manning J. Dauer, Clement H. Donovan and Gladys M. Kammerer. Gainesville, 1968.
iv, 44 p.

[Fl 33]
University of Florida. Public Administration Clearing Service.
   Proposed Amendments to the Florida Constitution, 1970 General Election. By Manning J. Dauer, Ernest R. Bartley and Thomas C. Marks, Jr. Gainesville, 1970 (Civic Information Series No. 50).
23 p.

[Fl 34]
University of Florida. Public Administration Clearing Service.
   Proposed Amendments to the Florida Constitution, March 14, 1972, Florida Election.
By Manning J. Dauer. Gainesville, 1972 (Civic Information Series No. 52).
13 p. manuscript

[Fl 35]
University of Florida. Public Administration Clearing Service.
   Proposed Amendments to the Florida Constitution and Bond Issue Referendum, Nov. 7,
1972, Florida Election. By Clement H. Donovan and Manning J. Dauer. Gainesville, 1972
(Civic Information Series No. 53).
18 p.

[Fl 36]
University of Florida. Public Administration Clearing Service.
   Proposed Amendments to the Florida Constitution, Nov. 5, 1974, Florida Election.
By Clement H. Donovan, Manning J. Dauer and Joseph W. Little. Gainesville, 1974 (Civic
Information Series No. 54).
18 p.

[Fl 37]
University of Florida. Public Administration Clearing Service.
   Amendment Providing Limited Taxing Power for Florida Regional Water Control
Districts. By Clement H. Donovan. Gainesville, 1976 (Civic Information Series No. 58).
7 p.

[Fl 41]
University of Florida. Bureau of Economic and Business Research.
   Economic Leaflets. Vol. XXV, no. 7, July 1966, "Finance and Taxation in the Proposed
Florida Constitution."
4 p.

[Fl 31]
Florida State University. Institute of Governmental Research (now Political Research Institute).
   Proposed Amendments to the Florida Constitution of 1885: An Analysis of Constitutional Amendment Proposals Presented to the Electorate Since 1885. Compiled by David F.
Dickson. Tallahassee, 1966.
87 p.

[Fl 38]
Florida State University. Institute for Governmental Research.
   Governmental Research Bulletin. Vol. II, No. 4, September 1965, "Constitutional Re-
vision: A Challenge to Floridians;" Vol. III, No. 2, March 1966, "Proposals to Amend
the 1885 Florida Constitution: Some Insights for Constitution Revision;" Vol. III, No. 5,
November 1966, "Florida's Universities and Constitutional Revision;" Vol. IV, No. 2,
March 1967, "The Florida Executive and Constitutional Revision."
24 p.

[Fl 40]
Florida State University. Institute for Governmental Research.
   Governmental Research Bulletin. Vol. IV, No. 3, May 1969, "The 1969 Florida Legislature: A New Constitution and the New Procedures."
4 p.

# Kentucky

NOTE: Kentucky. Legislative Research Commission.
   The Constitution of Kentucky, published, with an Explanatory Essay. By James T. Fleming. 6th edition. Frankfort, 1967 (Informational Bulletin 59).
xxiv, 49 p.
See Cynthia E. Browne, *State Constitutional Conventions From Independence to the Completion of the Present Union, 1776-1959: A Bibliography,* p. 76.
[Ky 10]

[Ky 11]
Kentucky. Legislative Research Commission.
   Kentucky's Constitutional Development. Frankfort, 1960 (Informational Bulletin No. 29).
20 p.

[Ky 12]
Kentucky. Legislative Research Commission. Constitution Revision Committee.
   You and Your Constitution . . . Kentucky Considers a Convention. Frankfort, July 1960.
(unpaged) 15 p.

[Ky 13]
Kentucky. Legislative Research Commission.
   The Constitution and Local Government. Frankfort, 1964. (Information Bulletin No. 36).
vii, 65 p.

[Ky 14]
Kentucky. Legislative Research Commission. Constitution Revision Committee.
   First Report of the Constitution Revision Committee to the Legislative Research Commission. Frankfort, 1960 (Research Report No. 2).
v, 51 p., biblio.

[Ky 15]
Kentucky. Legislative Research Commission.
   Summary of Constitution Revision Assembly Proposals. Frankfort, 1966 (Informational Bulletin No. 47).
ii, 14 p.

[Ky 16]
Kentucky. Legislative Research Commission.
  Proposed Revision of the Constitution of the Commonwealth of Kentucky. Submitted by the 1966 Kentucky General Assembly and Subject to Ratification by the Electorate on November 8, 1966. Frankfort, 1966 (Informational Bulletin No. 48).
28 p.

[Ky 17]
Kentucky. Legislative Research Bureau.
  A Comparison . . . The Present, the Proposed Kentucky Constitutions. Frankfort, 1966 (Informational Bulletin No. 52).
viii, 131 p.

# Louisiana

*NOTE:* See Susan Rice Yarger, *State Constitutional Conventions, 1959-1975: A Bibliography,* for other Public Affairs Research Council of Louisiana, Inc. Studies.

[La 38]
Public Affairs Research Council of Louisiana, Inc.
  PAR Conference – 1963: A New Approach to Constitutional Revision. Baton Rouge, April 1963 (PAR Analysis No. 111).
19 p.

[La 39]
Public Affairs Research Council of Louisiana, Inc.
  Citizen's Guide to the 1973 Constitutional Convention. Baton Rouge, April 1973.
58 p.

[La 40]
Public Affairs Research Council of Louisiana, Inc.
  Convention Commentary. Nos. 1-11. Baton Rouge, July-December 1973.
v.p., 109 p.

[La 41]
Public Affairs Research Council of Louisiana, Inc.
  Philosophies in the Proposed Constitution. Baton Rouge, February 1974 (PAR Analysis No. 196).
14 p.

[La 42]
Public Affairs Research Council of Louisiana, Inc.
  Special Election on the Constitution, April 20, 1974. Baton Rouge, April 1974 (PAR Analysis No. 198).
15 p.

[La 46]
Louisiana State University. Institute of Government Research.
  Focus on C-73. Baton Rouge, 1973.
163 p.

[La 44]
Louisiana. Constitutional Revision Commission.
   Memorandum to Committee on Rules and Procedure. Baton Rouge, 1970.
27 p.

[La 45]
Louisiana. Constitutional Revision Commission.
   First Report to the Louisiana Legislature. Baton Rouge, May 1971.
131 p.

[La 43]
Louisiana. Constitutional Convention.
   Proposed Rules of Procedure. Prepared by the Temporary Committee for Submission to the Convention. Baton Rouge, January 1973.
27 p.

# New Jersey

[NJ 23]
New Jersey. Governor.
  Special Message to the Legislature by Richard J. Hughes, Governor of New Jersey,
Trenton, November 30, 1964.
13 p.

[NJ 24]
New Jersey. Legislative Reapportionment and Congressional Redistricting Planning Commission. Report. Trenton, February 1965.
92 p., foldout maps.

[NJ 25]
New Jersey. Legislature.
  "An Act to provide for a constitutional convention . . . ." Chapter 33, P. L. 1965;
Senate Bill No. 261. Trenton, 1965.
10 p.
  "An Act to supplement 'An Act to provide for a constitutional convention . . . .' "
Senate Bill No. 369. Trenton, November 1965.
2 p.
  "An Act to amend 'An Act to provide for a constitutional convention . . . .' " Assembly
Bill No. 844. Trenton, January 1966.
2 p.
  "An Act to amend and supplement 'An Act to provide for a constitutional convention . .
. .' " Assembly Bill No. 373. Trenton, February 1966.
3 p.
(total 17 p.)

[NJ 28]
New Jersey. Constitutional Convention, 1966.
  Official Rules Adopted March 26, 1966: With List of Delegates, Committees, Officers
and Staff. New Brunswick, 1966.
vii, 45 p.

> *NOTE:* New Jersey. Constitutional Convention, 1966.
>   (Background Papers of the 1966 Constitutional Convention of the State of New
> Jersey. Trenton, 1966).
>   v.p.
>   See: Susan Rice Yarger, *State Constitutional Conventions, 1959-1975: A Bibliography,*
>   p. 35 [NJ 21]

[NJ 21A]
New Jersey. Constitutional Convention, 1966.
　(Background Papers - Supplement). Trenton, 1966. (Contents: "The Basis of Legislative
Reapportionment—Inhabitants, Citizens, Registered Voters, Actual Voters or Others").
14 p., biblio.

[NJ 26]
New Jersey. Constitutional Convention, 1966.
　Revision and Amendments to the State Constitution Relating to the Representation of
the People in the Legislature of This State, Agreed Upon By the Constitutional Convention
of 1966, To Be Submitted to the People for Their Approval or Rejection At the General
Election on November 8, 1966. Trenton, 1966.
4 p.

[NJ 27]
Brennan, William J.
　Report: Constitutional Reforms; Focus on Legislature. To New Jersey Bar Association.
(n.p.), February 1974.
18 p.

# Texas

[Tx 41]
Texas. Legislature Reference Library
  Constitutional Revision Materials available in the Legislative Reference Library. Prepared for the 1974 Texas Constitutional Convention. Compiled by Malinda Allison and Brenda Shelton, manuscript by Katherine Luscombe. Rev. Ed. Austin, December 1973.
87 p.

[Tx 43]
Texas Advisory Commission on Intergovernmental Relations.
  Amending the Texas Constitution: 1951-1972. By Janice C. May.
ix, 49 p.

[Tx 44]
Texas Advisory Commission on Intergovernmental Relations.
  Intergovernmental Issues in Constitutional Revision. Recommendations of the Texas Advisory Commission on Intergovernmental Relations. Austin, September 1973.
x, 31 p.

[Tx 45]
The University of Texas at Austin, Lyndon B. Johnson School of Public Affairs. The
  Constitution of Texas and the Administrative Structure of the State. Austin, 1973.
iv, 53 p.

[Tx 46]
The Texas Research League.
  A New Constitution for Texas?: Research on Revision. (n.p.), (n.d.).
24 p.

[Tx 47]
Texas Coastal and Marine Council.
  Constitutional Revision Issues. "Part I - Environmental Considerations," November 1973; "Part II - Energy and Transportation," December 1973. Austin, 1973.
13 p., 8 p.
(total 21 p.)

[Tx 60]
Common Cause of Texas.
  Telephone Opinion Survey: Texas Constitutional Revision - January 1974. Prepared by John Henson Associates. Austin, 1974.
11 p.

[Tx 48]
University of Houston. Institute for Urban Studies.
    The Texas Constitution and Its Impact -- An Annotated Bibliography. By Michael D.
Stevens and Kathleen Beatty. Houston, 1973.
50 p.

[Tx 49]
University of Houston. Institute for Urban Studies.
    The Impact of the Texas Constitution on Suffrage. By Del Taebel and Luther W. Odom.
Houston, 1973.
31 p., appendix.

[Tx 50]
University of Houston. Institute for Urban Studies.
    The Impact of the Texas Constitution on Natural Resources. By Jared E. Haxleton.
Houston, 1973.
61 p.

[Tx 51]
University of Houston. Institute for Urban Studies.
    The Impact of the Texas Constitution on Public Welfare. By Ruth A. Whiteside. Houston,
1973.
45 p.

[Tx 52]
University of Houston. Institute for Urban Studies.
    The Impact of the Texas Constitution on County Government. By Edwin Stene. Houston,
1973.
35 p.

[Tx 53]
University of Houston. Institute for Urban Studies.
    The Impact of the Texas Constitution on the Legislature. By The Citizens Conference
on State Legislatures. Houston, 1973.
57 p., bibliography.

[Tx 54]
University of Houston. Institute for Urban Studies.
    The Impact of the Texas Constitution on the Executive. By Fred Gantt, Jr. Houston, 1973.
v. p., 158 p.

[Tx 55]
University of Houston. Institute for Urban Studies.
    The Impact of the Texas Constitution on the Criminal Justice System. By Allan K.
Butcher, James W. Stevens and Gloria W. Eyres. Houston, 1973.
222 p.

[Tx 56]
University of Houston. Institute for Urban Studies.
    Impact of the Texas Constitution on the Judiciary. By Allen E. Smith. Houston, 1973.
125 p.

[Tx 57]
University of Houston. Institute for Urban Studies.
   The Impact of the Texas Constitution on Education. By Irving Dawson, John Thompson and Fred Waddell. Houston, 1973.
51 p., appendices, bibliography

[Tx 58]
University of Houston. Institute for Urban Studies.
   The Texas Constitution: Its Impact on the Administration. By Emmette S. Redford. Houston, 1973.
113 p., appendices.

[Tx 42]
University of Houston. Institute for Urban Studies.
   Texas Public Policy Notes. Vol. 1, no. 2 - "Proposed Article III: The Legislature," August 1975.; Vol. 1, no. 4 - "State and Local Finance Implications of the Proposed Constitution," October 1975. Houston, 1975.
10 p., 8 p.
(total 18 p.)

[Tx 59]
Texas. Council of Presidents, Public Senior Colleges and Universities and Committee on Governing Boards, Public Senior Colleges and Universities.
   Recommendations Concerning Article VII, Education, of a Proposed Constitution for Texas: Presented to the 63rd Legislature Sitting as a Constitutional Convention - 1974. (n.p.), November 26, 1973.
27 p.

[Tx 67]
Texas. Constitutional Revision Commission.
   Resource Documents Notebooks for the Constitutional Revision Commission. Convention Resource Notebook. Austin, 1973.
unpaged (370 p.)

[Tx 68]
———. Committee on the Legislative Branch.
unpaged (400 p.)

[Tx 69]
———. Committee on the Executive Branch.
unpaged (459 p.)

[Tx 70]
———. Committee on the Judiciary. Vols. I & II.
unpaged (389p., 234 p.)

[Tx 71]
———. Committee on Rights, Suffrage, Amendment, and Separation of Powers.
unpaged (80 p.)

[Tx 72]
———. Committee on Education. Vols. I & II.
unpaged (270 p., 285 p.)

[Tx 73]
———. Committee on Finance. Vols. I, II & III.
unpaged (401 p., 343 p,, 275 p.)

[Tx 74]
———. Committee on Local Government.
unpaged (298 p.)

[Tx 75]
———. Committee on General Provisions.
unpaged (326 p.)

> NOTE: Texas. Constitutional Revision Commission.
> A New Constitution for Texas. Prepared by the Commission. Austin, 1973.
> vii, 51 p.
> See: Susan Rice Yarger, *State Constitutional Conventions, 1959-1975: A Bibliography*,
> p. 50 [Tx 33] .

[Tx 77]
Texas. Constitutional Revision Commission.
Detailed Subject Index of "A New Constitution for Texas" As Proposed by the Texas
Constitutional Revision Commission. By Ione Stumberg. (n.p.), (n.d.).
65 p.

> NOTE: Texas. Joint Constitutional Convention Planning Commission.
> Proposed Rules of Procedure: 1974 Texas Constitutional Convention. Austin, 1971.
> (3), 72 p.
> See: Susan Rice Yarger, *State Constitutional Conventions, 1959-1975: A Bibliography*,
> p. 49 [Tx 28] .

> NOTE: Texas. Joint Constitutional Convention Planning Commission.
> Staff Reports: 1974 Texas Constitutional Convention. Austin, 1974.
> iii, 52 p.
> See: Susan Rice Yarger, *State Constitutional Conventions, 1959-1975: A Bibliography*,
> p. 50 [Tx 37]

[Tx 61]
Texas Constitutional Convention.
Constitutional Convention of Texas: Procedures Manual. (n.p.), (n.d.).
41 p.

[Tx 62]
Texas Constitutional Convention.
The Constitutional Convention of 1974: Rules of Procedure. Constitutional Convention
Resolution No. 4. Austin, Adopted January 10, 1974.
78 p.

[Tx 63]
Texas Constitutional Convention, 1974.
Record of Proceedings: Official Journals. January 8, 1974-July 30, 1974. Vols. I & II.
Austin, (n.d.).
2654 p.

[Tx 64]
Texas Constitutional Convention, 1974.
  Record of Proceedings: Official Journals. January 8, 1974-July 30, 1974. Vols I & II.
Austin (n.d.).
2113 p.

[Tx 65]
Texas. Secretary of State.
  Proposed Constitution of the State of Texas. Austin, 1974.
23 p.

[Tx 76]
Texas Legislative Council. Office of Constitutional Research.
  Constitutional Amendments Analyzed: Analysis of the Eight Proposed Amendments
for Election - November 4, 1975. Austin, 1975.
49 p.

[Tx 79]
Office of Constitutional Research.
  Revising the Texas Constitution. 1972-1975. Austin, January 1976.
v.p., 530 l.

[Tx 78]
Office of Constitutional Research.
  Methods of Constitutional Revision in Texas. January 1976.
v.p., 325 l.

[Tx 66]
Texas. Legislature.
  Informational Booklet on the Proposed 1976 Revision of the Texas Constitution.
Austin, (n.d.).
129 p.

# Washington

[Wa 28]
Washington. Secretary of State.
   Amendments to the State Constitution. (n.p.), 1966.
16 p.

[Wa 9]
Washington. Bureau of Governmental Research and Services.
   Washington State Constitution - Stumbling Block or Stepping Stone? Proceedings of the Thirty-first Annual Summer Institute of Government, University of Washington. Seattle, November 1966 (Report No. 162).
79 p.

[Wa 10]
Washington. Bureau of Governmental Research and Services.
   Washington's Constitutional Dilemma. Proceedings of the Conference, October 15, 1966, University of Washington. Seattle, March 1967 (Report No. 164).

[Wa 13]
Washington. Constitutional Advisory Council.
   Report. (n.p.), December 1966.
27 p., bibliography

[Wa 11]
Washington. Steering Committee on Constitutional Reform.
   Washington Looks at Constitutional Reform: A Background Prepared for the Steering Committee on Constitutional Reform. (n.p.), 1967.
36 l., xxix, bibliography (total 69 l.)

[Wa 26]
Washington State Division, American Association of University Women. A Constitution for the State of Washington. (n.p.), 1967.
27 p.

[Wa 25]
Washington. State Constitutional Revision Conference.
   (Proceedings.) June 13-14, 1968. Sponsored by University of Washington School of Law. Seattle, 1968.
v.p. (228 l.)

[Wa 27]
Washington. Constitutional Revision Committee (Commission?)
    Report to Governor Daniel J. Evans. (n.p.), October 19, 1967.
9 p.

[Wa 14]
Washington (State) Constitutional Revision Commission, 1968-1969.
    Draft Reports. November 15, 1968 and April 29, 1969. Compiled by Ralph Johnson
for Constitutional Revision Seminar, Law School, University of Washington. Seattle, 1969.
v.p. (total 374 l.)

> CONTENTS: "Washington's Constitution: Interim Report of the Constitutional
> Revision Commission" 6 p.; "Drafts and Revisions of the Final Report," 38 l.;
> "Minutes," 57 l.; "Memos," 31 l.; "Gateway" (revision amendment), 21 l.;
> "Elections," 5 l.; "Executive," 38 l.; "Education," 13 l.; "Legislative," 35 l.;
> "Judicial," 36 l.; "Initiative, Referendum, and Recall," 30 l.; "Local Government,"
> 13 l.; "Report to Governor, November 15, 1968," 44 l." "Outline of Constitution,"
> 10 l.

[Wa 15]
Washington. Constitutional Revision Commission.
    Final Report to Governor Daniel J. Evans. (n.p.), June 1969.
93 l.

[Wa 12]
University of Washington, School of Law.
    Constitutional Revision in Washington: Legal Aspects. Papers prepared by students,
edited by Ralph W. Johnson. Seattle (?), 1970.
v.p. (total 304 l.)

[Wa 16]
Washington. Commission for Constitutional Alternatives.
    (Papers). Olympia, 1975-1976.
v.p. (total 20 p.)

> CONTENTS: Executive order creating commission: joint resolution calling
> for constitutional convention; House Bill No. 1328 - "An Act relating
> to a state constitutional convention . . . ;" "Constitutional Amendments -
> Year and Subject Matter;" Keynote address - Commission for Constitutional
> Alternatives. November 15, 1975.

[Wa 17]
Washington. Commission for Constitutional Alternatives.
    Constitutional Convention––Washington State, 1975: A Study of the History of
Constitutional Revision in Washington State and a Synopsis of Constitutional Convention
Experiences in Ten Other States. Prepared by Mary Ellen Hudgins. Olympia, 1975.
21 l., bibliography

[Wa 18]
Washington. Commission for Constitutional Alternatives.
    An Analysis of Washington State's Constitution and Possible Alternatives to Its
Existing Articles: a Working Paper (excerpts). Prepared by Sally E. Mathiasen.
Olympia, August 1975.
15 l.

[Wa 19]
Washington. Commission for Constitutional Alternatives.
 Washington's Constitution: A Time for Rebuilding. Olympia, November 1975.
(unpaged) 13 l.

[Wa 20]
Washington. Commission for Constitutional Alternatives.
 Previous Commissions' Findings: A Summary. Prepared by John C. Marks. Olympia,
December 1975.
18 l.

[Wa 21]
Washington. Commission for Constitutional Alternatives.
 Methods for Revision of the State Constitution. Prepared by John C. Marks. Olympia,
December 1975.
12 p.

[Wa 22]
Washington. Commission for Constitutional Alternatives.
 Citizen Concerns and Constitutional Issues. Prepared by John C. Marks. Olympia,
January 1976.
4 l.

[Wa 23]
Washington. Commission for Constitutional Alternatives.
 Costs and State Constitutional Conventions. Prepared by Stacey J. Hendrickson. Olympia,
August 1975.

[Wa 24]
Washington. Commission for Constitutional Alternatives.
 Citizen Ideas and Information Needs Regarding a Constitutional Convention. Prepared
by Communication Design. Seattle, January 1976.
4 p.

# Wisconsin

[Wi 23]
Wisconsin. Commission on Constitutional Revision.
  A Report to the Governor. Madison, 1960.
17 p.

[Wi 24]
University of Wisconsin. Bureau of Government.
  County Government and the Constitution: A Report to the County Government
Committee of the Wisconsin Legislative Council. (n.p.), November 1960.
40 p.

[Wi 7]
League of Women Voters of Wisconsin.
  Constitutional Problems and Constitutional Change. Madison, February 1962.
19 p.

[Wi 8]
Wisconsin. Legislative Reference Bureau.
  Proposed Constitutional Amendments and Referendum to Be Submitted to the
Wisconsin Voters at the April 7, 1964, Election. Madison, February 1964 (Informational
Bulletin No. 64-4).
14 p.

[Wi 9]
Wisconsin. Legislative Reference Bureau.
  Implementing the Recommendations of the Commission on Constitutional Revision
Submitted to the Governor in December 1960. Madison, October 1964 (Brief 64-6).
15 p.

[Wi 10]
Wisconsin. Legislative Reference Bureau.
  Constitutional Revision in Wisconsin. Madison, May 1965 (Research Bulletin 65-2).
56 p., index

[Wi 11]
Wisconsin. Legislative Reference Bureau.
  Organization and Procedures of a Constitutional Convention. Madison, May 1965 (Research
Bulletin 65-4).

[Wi 12]
Wisconsin. Legislative Reference Bureau.
   Constitutional Amendment Proposals, Successful and Unsuccessful: 1961 to 1965
Wisconsin Legislatures. Madison, October 1966 (Research Bulletin 66-5).
41 p., index

[Wi 13]
Wisconsin. Legislative Reference Bureau.
   Constitutional Amendments to be Submitted to the Wisconsin Electorate, April 1967.
Madison, March 1967 (Informational Bulletin 67-5).
11 p.

[Wi 14]
Wisconsin. Legislative Reference Bureau.
   Constitutional Amendments to be Submitted to the Wisconsin Electorate, April 2, 1968.
Madison, March 1968 (Brief 68-1).
9 p.

[Wi 15]
Wisconsin. Legislative Reference Bureau.
   Constitutional Amendments and Referenda to be Submitted to the Wisconsin Electorate,
April 1, 1969. Madison, March 1969 (Information Bulletin 69-1).

[Wi 16]
Wisconsin. Legislative Reference Bureau.
   Constitutional Amendments to be Submitted to the Wisconsin Electorate, April 4, 1972.
Madison, February 1972 (Informational Bulletin 72-1).
17 p.

[Wi 17]
Wisconsin. Legislative Reference Bureau.
   Disposition of Constitutional Amendment Proposals: 1961-1971 Wisconsin Legislatures.
Madison, April 1972 (Research Bulletin 72-4).

[Wi 18]
Wisconsin. Legislative Reference Bureau.
   Constitutional Amendments to be Submitted to the Wisconsin Electorate, April 3, 1973.
Madison, March 1973 (Informational Bulletin 73-1).
13 p.

[Wi 19]
Wisconsin. Legislative Reference Bureau.
   Constitutional Amendments to be Submitted to the Wisconsin Electorate, April 2, 1974.
Madison, March 1974 (Brief 74-2).
9 p.

[Wi 20]
Wisconsin. Legislative Reference Bureau.
   Constitutional Amendments to be Submitted to the Wisconsin Electorate, April 1, 1975.
Madison, March 1975 (Brief 75-2).
10 p.

[Wi 21]
Wisconsin. Legislative Reference Bureau.
   Constitutional Amendments to be Submitted to the Wisconsin Electorate, April 6, 1976.
Madison, March 1976 (Brief 76-2).
7 p.

[Wi 22]
Wisconsin. Legislative Reference Bureau.
  Wisconsin Constitution as Amended April 1, 1975. Madison, July 1975 (Informational
Bulletin 75-IB-4).

# Index

Publisher's Note: Subjects are referenced under each state by Fiche number and documents page. A page designation, "1," indicates that the subject is covered throughout the document; an * indicates that the document has no pagination.

| *Administration* | page |
| --- | --- |
| Louisiana | |
| La 40, no. 9 | 1 |
| La 41 | 10 |
| Texas | |
| Tx 45 | 1 |
| Tx 58 | 1 |
| Wisconsin | |
| Wi 7 | 6 |
| Wi 10 | 41 |
| Wi 16 | 5 |
| Wi 17 | 86 |
| Wi 19 | 1 |
| Wi 23 | 1 |

| *Amendment Process* (s.n.: method in which the Constitution may be amended) | |
| --- | --- |
| California | |
| Ca 32 | 105 |
| Ca 49 | 1 |
| Ca 65 | 1 |
| Delaware | |
| De 41 | 2552 |
| Florida | |
| Fl 27 | 26 |
| Fl 29 | 1 |
| General Publications | |
| GP 3 | 9 |
| GP 3 | 28 |
| Texas | |
| Tx 43 | 1 |
| Tx 67 | * |
| Tx 71 | * |

| Washington | page |
| --- | --- |
| Wa 22 | 4 |
| Wisconsin | |
| Wi 7 | 8 |
| Wi 8 | 7 |
| Wi 10 | 10 |
| Wi 10 | 48 |
| Wi 17 | 77 |
| Wi 23 | 2 |
| Wi 23 | 4 |

| *Amendments* (s.n.: actual amendments to the Constitution) | |
| --- | --- |
| Florida | |
| Fl 30 | 1 |
| Fl 31 | 1 |
| Fl 32 | 39 |
| Fl 39 | 1 |
| Kentucky | |
| Ky 11 | 14 |
| Washington | |
| Wa 11 | 34 |
| Wa 11 | xiv |
| Wa 15 | 30 |
| Wa 15 | 79 |
| Wa 28 | 1 |
| Wisconsin | |
| Wi 8 | 1 |
| Wi 10 | 22 |
| Wi 12 | 1 |
| Wi 13 | 1 |
| Wi 14 | 1 |
| Wi 15 | 1 |